O Lady, Speak Again

O Lady, Speak Again

poems by

Dayna Patterson

SIGNATURE BOOKS | 2023 | SALT LAKE CITY

Design by Jason Francis

© 2023 Signature Books. Published by arrangement with the
copyright holder. All rights reserved. Signature Books is a registered
trademark of Signature Books Publishing, LLC.

www.signaturebooks.com

FIRST EDITION | 2023

LIBRARY OF CONGRESS CONTROL NUMBER: 2022948757

Paperback ISBN: 978-1-56085-464-7
Ebook ISBN: 978-1-56085-481-4

For Nana & Kim & my daughters—fire-speakers.

Who is't that goes with me? Beseech your highness
My women may be with me, for you see
My plight requires it.
—*The Winter's Tale*

She is more at home on the fringes than in the center.
... Intrinsically ambivalent and polymorphous,
she straddles conventional boundaries and eludes definition.
—*Oxford Classical Dictionary*

Contents

III

IV

Dramatis Personae

Miranda. Cordelia. Ophelia. Isabella. *O lady, speak again.*

Hermione and Perdita. Jessica and Portia. Viola and Olivia. Desdemona. *O lady, speak again.*

Lady Macbeth and the Three Witches. Paulina. Juliet and her Nurse. Titania. Mistress Page and Mistress Ford. Rosalind. *O lady, speak again.*

&

Speak, from Latin *spargere*, to sprinkle, to scatter.

Parched in dry earth. Speak—*again*—the first time partial, unquenching.

Sprinkle, scatter a blue deluge.

&

Stepping over the threshold of silence, divide Self into selves, braid my stories into theirs. Stories rooted in Mormon soil, in the desert of Deseret. Stories of being raised in a Motherless house, launching toward horizon's grey smudge. Stories of the underdog's spellsong, its fluid music, speaking.

&

O lady, speak again. Replace *end* with *and*. Amend, upend, augment, reinvent, retell, unveil, expound, expatiate, chide, upbraid. Sound off and sound deep. Hail and hold. Spout and spiel and speak.

Dayna Patterson

Thunder. Enter the three WITCHES meeting HECATE

Invoke her at your thresh-
hold, holy daughter of Nyx. Worker
from afar, *hekatos*. Queen

of Ghosts. Paint her on your lintel, liminal god-
dess, choosy protectoress, a fist-
ful of blessing to bestow.

Or withhold. Doldrums, or wind in the sail. Her herald:
a choral whine and howl. Her familiars:
a black bitch and a polecat. Spectral

at the place where roads cross, three-
bodied, or three-headed body—horsehead, dog-
head, lionhead. A mouth of moan, plea-

sure and pain. Tri-plicit-ous she, full moon, half
moon, new moon. Virgin and mother, mystery
-cowled daughter. Weave a wreath of yew, garlic, bella-

donna, mandrake. At the town wall's portcullis,
at the fortress's gate, she holds
daggers and torches, keys and snakes.

Tri
-morph
-ous.

From her cave she hears a daughter's
distress, leads mother to omnivoyant light
and chthonic dark. Her credo: *Round, around,*

around, about,
about. Leave her a sacrifice of black
female lambs, of honey, of dogs, her

sacrament. Psychopomp. Eternity's stitcher. Soul-
threader. Build her a shrine at the en-
trance.

I

I live in a Motherless house.
—Carol Lynn Pearson

Self-Portrait as Miranda after Shipwreck

Many have identified Mormon church rhetoric on LGBT issues in the years following California Proposition 8 in 2008 and especially in the wake of the 2015 Supreme Court ruling as a potential cause of the uptick in youth suicides in Utah compared to the rest of the country.
—Benjamin Knoll, *The Huffington Post*, 2016

And many saints there were who made shipwreck of their faith.
—Charles Ramsden Bailey
(my great-great-great grandfather), 1877

Father entreats me not to see   topsail thrashed

wreckage of rock-ripped ship   the sailors' keen *we split   we split*

we split!   breathshorn in brack and brine

uncanny lightning   airy fire fissures

cracking the squall of blue-black storm   *O the cry did knock*

against my very heart   harrowing   He tells me *no harm done   No harm*

cease your worry   sits me down to recount the story of how

we drifted to this

isolate   island where   in the time before

I was princess   He was Duke   *a prince of power*

of a pre-island place not unfraught with turmoil

He promises no one lost   not one hair   of those I heard cry

those I saw sink

and soon

we'll spirit away, lay claim to our inheritance   when we leave

soon   hush   he tush-tushes and sluices me   to heaviness

where I dream   goldenglow streets   blood blemished

and Father's footstep thunders   and Ariel's voice sings

full fathom five thy father   *lies*

I harbor their cries knocking   still

O is the Sound of Tragedy

O as in Romeo's doomed
romance, as in Juliet's hopeless wound
O for the little moan in Desdemona, alpha and omega
of Othello,   noose at the end of Iago   O as the coward
in Antony, whose autodestruct proved too slow   O of Cleopatra's
poison, the coiled asp of her final show   As in Lear's *Blow, winds, and crack*
your cheeks! Rage! Blow!   his crawl toward old   O as in woe, open-mouth
circle,   hole in our faces,   exit of groans,   flow where flies or food may go
My mother's float   My father's snow   My faith in the whole,   holy,   wholly
broke O for the gone in Goneril O as in go, run, revoke the order for Cordelia's—
oh no O for the double O's of Gloucester's eyes, the twin O's in look, which he can't
because O is for *Out, vile jelly!* O as in mold, fold, follow folly, fall into nothing, no
thing, to zero O as in globe, *rotundity of the world*, loaded with the O of sorrow O
probes and prones *look Look look Look* to *see so much*, and know O says
no, no, no life   no breath   no more   ghost   poor fool   undo
O for ambition's goad, for the smoke of Macbeth's unholy goal
O for Ophelia drowned, for Hamlet's lost crown,
his dying throes,   his *O, I die, Horatio,*
his *O, O, O, O*

In this version

Romeo doesn't drink the apothecary's poison,
and Juliet awakens in his arms. They ride
horseback to Mantua and have seven kids,
hyphenate their surnames: Montague-Capulet.

Hamlet checks behind the hangings, sword sheathed,
and Ophelia doesn't drown in the glassy brook,
but goes to a women's college, studies botany.
Fratricidal uncle-king, guilt-gutted, offs himself.

In this version, Lear doesn't banish his third girl,
and Cordelia cares for him in second childhood,
spooning mashed turnip to his lips when teeth fail.
Cradles his head as he slips into void.

Othello suspects his suspicions, suffocates
his doubts, crushes the spine of Iago's lie,
loosens the villain's tongue so he finally explains.
And Desdemona bears cinnamon twins.

The nursling lives, and Lady Macbeth, Thane's wife,
is queenly, but not queen. Is content with legacy,
only nightwalking to hush her infant's teething,
only brewing wild poppy & milk for its gums.

In this version, I chase away my mother's blue beasts,
concoct a strong spell to keep her from breaking
out of my childhood. Later when I break
from my father's faith, fissures don't shift to ravines.

Leontes believes Hermione, or better yet
he never succumbs to morbid jealousy.
Therefore, their Perdita grows up like a song,
her mother's face familiar as sun on her skin.

Dayna Patterson

Self-Portrait as Cordelia, Mormon Polygamous Wife

*And I say if Plurel Marrige or Celestial Marrige is not true then
Mormonasim is all a oacks.*
—Charles Ramsden Bailey, my great-great-great grandfather

*Meantime we shall express our darker purpose. ... Know that we
have divided in three our kingdom.*
—King Lear

I.

Delia, he calls me,
as if his mouth were too full of names
to twine the full of mine around his tongue.

We are trefoil clover, latched to the same
stem, fixing nitrogen, converting it to the stuff of life,
but now I've become the tear-away leaf.

Far from my husband's affection—
Third, the put-away wife,
distant as rooster from roasted hen.

He used to hold me close, proud
of my lace, my waves of lavender-scented hair,
the crisp of my bun and starched linens,

the way I can make a meal of a willow branch,
boiled pigweed and thistle greens, corn cake,
or a skillet of sego lily bulbs,

the way I churn out son after son
like pads of stamped butter
with his milky impression.

II.

Then, my niggling questions surfaced—
Why Father Son Spirit, a male-only guild
for a godhead? And is Father the Great Polygamist

with many goddess-wives? And
why not prophetesses in Zion, Miriams
and Deborahs and Annas?

I let slip from the pantry
the mouse of my doubts, let its warm brown
scurry into the open, and find myself

shelved, long-languishing in a rough valley.
Chicory and bitter herbs in my garden grow
parched under desert sun.

Come harvest, I'll glean grain enough to sell,
sew a dress of linsey-woolsey,
dye the cloth with rabbit brush for yellow,

then indigo for a summer green to reap
again his gaze. Or maybe I'll begin
with madder and a mordant, less likely to fade.

III.

He frequents First Wife now,
enlarged her log house
with an upstairs room.

I who care for him know
she's low-burning coal
in a brazier about to spill,

a hearth flame without a screen,
embers and ash wafting in the updraft.
What she touches, she incinerates.

Second Wife's a cowhide copy
branded with First Wife's spite.
I didn't swallow in marrying him, I'd sister-wife

them. Both have that *glib and oily art*
of Pharisees, all whited sepulchers
with rotting bones beneath.

I may as well be in another country,
far from his favor and broken faith.
Love, and be silent.

I expect we'll still—all of us—share a grave.

And Why Not Change the Story?

Shakespeare certainly did.
In his sources, Juliet was 16.
He made her 13,
just shy of a sonnet.

And as to Macbeth's regicidal plot,
Banquo was the accomplice,
not Lady Macbeth, a ten-year's queen
next to her prosperous husband-king.

Billy-Boy plagiarized and revised the stories,
so why not change his?
Grow a patch of clover
or a thicket of wild allspice,
where now a grave is.

Self-Portrait as Miranda, A Green Girl

How lush and lusty the grass looks! how green!
— The Tempest

Jungle	I gather grass from the lawn,
Juniper	gob my cheeks, chew and chew
Chartreuse	and chew, hoping for grape,
Lime	watermelon. A neighbor girl, Ariel
Kelly	tells me if I chew long enough, it will turn
Sweetgrass	into gum. I was the kind of kid
Casino	who stole from Dad's giant jar of loose change,
Bottle	the stash he kept in a corner of his room
Whisper	where he slept like an island
Envy	on his king-sized waterbed.
Grasshopper	I'd skip half a mile to the store where gallon
Seafoam	wide-mouths cast a saccharine spell:
Pear	raspberries, red fish, gummy worms,
Apple	lemon sours, jawbreakers, a penny apiece.
Seaweed	If caught, I'd lie and tell him
Parakeet	I found a quarter in the parking lot
Pickle	or in the dry ditch or the grass.
Moss	My lie goes down like a tome in ocean.

Olive	He could do most magic but this—
Jade	call me out of my sugar ache.
Emerald	Perhaps, marooned, he didn't really want to.
Crocodile	That grass I chew and chew until,
Verdigris	teeth green, I spit the wad, dribbling
Viridian	into the dirt. It looks like gum.
Sage	Had she not lied after all?

Anagnorisis—in the Green Room

shield of fictive skin / paper thin / wardrobe the heart and clone

each scar / each wound's seethe / salved / dressed clean

cloister close / don't come out / yet cocoon of tunic doublet lace

don't the fabric folds / fit nice the words / an easy-flowing out

how / comfortable the mask / against my face / fiction better

barrier than none / cloak my part / paint each scar each / wound's garnet

portrait / wait for the signal sign / -seeker wait / for a wedding /
    a wandering star

Self-Portrait of Isabella as Mormon Middle Child

I.

One by one within a month, four siblings bring their grievances before
Father, ruler of our domain. The laws of the home are too strict, they
complain, no gum in the house—let alone sex or booze. No shoes on the
living room's cream carpet. A three-hour dose of church Sunday morning,
an hour of seminary each day. They prefer to smoke pot, join debate
club, practice hot words on the walls of our home, fire bombs smashing
windows. They drink and fuck and play angry guitars in the garage,
dip tube socks in gasoline, light them, slingshot flaming baby gerbils,
rodent rockets, over the backyard fence. They raise geckos, garter snakes,
an albino rat they shoot in the head when it escapes and eats a litter of
gerbils. They hyperbolize to shock, say they've tried heroin, crack, watch
Father crumble to new resolve, his whiplash no longer lax. Laws no more
a scarecrow where birds perch, forgetting terror. He cuts them off, clips
their wings, hurls them into future.

II.

I cloister myself in my room, like a Mormon nun,
except there's no such thing. I want strict restraint,
wake before sunrise to walk to seminary,
mark up my scriptures to a rainbow
of Godwords, praise dads from the pulpit, determined
to balm Father's disappointment, to foil the failures
of all my siblings, the sin of coffee far off
as Australia, the sin of sex distant as Saturn
with its chastity belt. I would be a ring of ice rock,
snowbroth blood. I would have God's name
in my mouth to chew on, my sustenance to savor,

a night-and-day saint with my symbols: a vase of milk
-white porcelain with blooming sego,
a golden liahona, compass with needle to arrow
the Godward path I'd follow. I'd place on the altar 18
months of my life, missionary away the days
knocking on doors shut like coffin lids,
wading through thigh-deep noes. I would marry
in a crenellated holy temple my first kiss.
I would sing hymns and hymns to Him,
force my voice *forte*: louder, louder, loud
enough to shake down angels.

Self-Portrait as Isabella in Theophilic Ecstasy

I want   warm convent caress   more
bead fingers I want   chaplet thwacking my thigh I want
                                       the lash of Christlove

more

Give,
and it shall be given unto you good measure, pressed down, and shaken
together, and running over shall men give into your bosom

the veil between us torn I want   a pedestal a petal a peal
cherubim wings aflutter

                                       more

Bell me, Christ the Clapper   Beat, ring, a three hour's
                                       campanology

                                       my fields ablaze I want

surrender
                    strait is the gate, and narrow is the way
white fruit luminous
fruit fire fruit expurgate my vile

                                       till I'm a crisp, clean, ironed

Sabbath day

virtue polished   *For with the same measure*
seraphim-scented   *that ye mete withal*
holiness washed and combed   *it shall be measured to you again*

I want   fingers   closing from above
(me)   polish this thurible

incense smoke

vesper vapor raising

from rose garland to thorn
white to St. Clare's brown

crown   from bride's

an armful of early hours

pink   rose   white

a bed of light

Self-Portrait as Ophelia in 33 Hues of Blewe

Indigo   *in the beginning was*   Woad   *Enter Ghost*

Midnight   Mothergone   Blood   Fathergod   Palatinate

my king-bound county   Lapis Lazuli   *speak like a green girl*

Gunmetal   lost by childlight   Ultramarine   mum in the inter-

regnum   Navy   lost by fishlight   Monastral   immersion

baptismal   Dark   *mermaid-like*   Pthalo   *The woman will be*

out   Zaffre   a ghost heart   Cobalt   pulsing porcelain

Medium   *It would be spoke to*   Giotto   a cock crows   Violet

a toy in blood   Deep Sky   *sweet, not lasting*   True

The rain it raineth   Azure   *every day*   Cerulean

sugar over the devil   Royal   *with a larger tether may he*

Glacier   all my orisons   Electric   by eel light

Cyan   dram of hebenon   Celeste   by ice light   Bassinet

think yourself a   Baby   *We know what we are*   Liberty

but not what we may be   Powder   owl daughter   Rue

a suit of sables   Sky   by skylight   Light   *Exit Ghost*

Self-Portrait as Jessica with Phoropter and Ursa Minor

I.

It was like following a map
that line by line erased itself
until one day it showed blank.

It was a compass that failed
a little more by the month
till it simply spun circles.

It was a daily change of glasses
fluctuating strength
so that vision fishbowled.

North Star, I could not find.
It dissipated, dissolved,
white heat into day's white,

in blankness left me blind.

II.

If I had left a note when I eloped in the night,
it might have said: Dear Father,
my loss is not yours to hold
like a handful of glass slivers.

There are too many ways to say
I'm sorry without returning to the fold,
without remitting the chest of jewels and ducats
I'll have already spent, your years of investment.

My sorries would all be holding
their breaths. I beg you not to make a fist,
needling shards in. I am what you raised
and will always be what I am.

If you want to blame my husband or Mom, long gone,
know I will step into the gondola
on my own without his steadying
hand, without her

ghostlight. But I'll keep her ring,
the turquoise, remembering
how you wouldn't trade it
for *a wilderness of monkeys.*

And although I'm no longer with you,
know this—
I'm not quite anywhere
else.

Self-Portrait of Jessica as
Mormon Meeting House, Repurposed

Hear you me, Jessica:
Lock up my doors; ...
... stop my house's ears
—Jessica's father, Shylock,
The Merchant of Venice

be of good cheer, for truly I think you are damned
— The Merchant of Venice

I.

I used to sit squirmy in a plastic row to memorize
Articles of Faith, all thirteen ingrained on fleshy
tables, but I've unstopped my house's ears, thrown open
casements, unlocked doors to memory's architects
and vandals, every other word now razed—

We believe in   ,   ,
and in   ,   ,
and in   Holy   .

Stolen, the old Fribergs, Nephi's muscled arm outstretched
to rebuke the rebellious. In their stead, squares of pale
patch the halls, a ghost gallery.

Interstellar maps graffiti distance between this galaxy
and godlessness. In lieu of Michelangelo's Sistine heaven,
evolution slow-prods Homo erectus.

We believe in being honest, true,   ,
benevolent,   , and in doing good to all   ;
.

                              anything   , lovely, or of good report
or praiseworthy,   seek after these   .

II.

In the chapel, lustrous brass organ pipes
still line the altar wall, and when the wind sweeps
through flung-open windows
across their waiting mouths,
hear the haunt of hymns—

We'll find the place   ,
Far away, in the West,
Where none shall come to hurt or make afraid;
There the saints, will be   .

Arched windows flood with shine and highlight
a massive portrait left hanging—a pioneer in forget-me-not
blue, baby in arms, a covered wagon's hulk
looming behind her like a domestic beast,
prairie guardian seagulls wheeling in her wake. I name her:
Madonna of Sagebrush. Goddess of the West.

We'll make the air, with music ring,
Shout praises   ;
                    these words we'll tell—
            !   !

III.

And here the balcony pew where my father gave me
my first set of scriptures bound in white pleather,
my name embossed in cursive silver. The echo of teachers'
voices, pressing: *Insert yourself in the first verse—*

I,   , having been born of goodly parents,
therefore I was taught somewhat
in all the learning
of my father

In the basement, the footprint of the baptismal font
ripped out, where my father dipped me under
a chlorine skin to bleach me clean, before I could pinch
my nose, before I could seal myself
a breath, and I inhaled water.

I baptize you in the name
of the Father,
and of   ,
and of

Self-Portrait as Miranda, Reminiscent

I didn't know how much I would miss
    the sound of the sea, the freedom
        to strip where I pleased, leave my clothes in a heap

on a piece of driftwood, and ease my body
    into green water. I miss the slip of seaweed,
        marine bracelets lacing my arms and legs, and the harsh

cry of seagulls, the echo of my blood
   hidden beneath a flared shell's lip.

This brave new world is a gallimaufry
of sweaty mobs, and market silks,
turquoise and tangerine, the smell
of piss from emptied chamber pots,
reeking narrow cobblestone streets,
and a hodgepodge of spice, saffron
and sage. It is whiplash with wonder
and ends with every third thought bent
towards an underground bed.

In my dreams I circle back to the strand,
    wade affably past eelgrass,
        nudge aside stingrays with my careful shuffle,

wind and water spritzing my skin as I go in
    to recover heavy spell books drowned,
        their vellum enchanted so I can still make out

my father's marginalia, his faithful calligraphy,
    illuminations in gold leaf.

II

Liminal. A threshold. My body between worlds.
... We are born from what is fluid, not fixed.
Water is essential. A mother is essential.
—Terry Tempest Williams

Hermione in Prison

When I married a lion,

        I should have expected teeth
        at my throat, my head
        in his mouth, paws
        pinning hands to the dirt.

Stripped of my purple,

        trampled.
        Gutted and guttered.
        My good name orphaned,
        I can neither see nor hear

my children like ghosts

        from inside this rat hole.
        My newborn girl,
        cord cut in cell's squalor,
        is our too young ambassador,

mitigating war between

        estranged countries. I'm afraid
        she's lost to me. I didn't know
        these stone walls interlock without mortar—
        not even my night screams breach

their tight lips.

        Bribing guards, friends bring offerings:
        Lady's bedstraw for the fleas.
        Cabbage leaves to draw out the milk.
        Fresh rags. If only there were a salve

for my vivisected heart,

                              I would pry open the jail
                              of my ribs to apply it.
                              My veins run dry.
                              Oh, Paulina,

sister, I'm hollow,

                              harrowed, rent.
                              Tell the lion
                              there is no more blood
                              to lap up.

Self-Portrait of Perdita as Lost I

start somewhere / start lost / re / member mother

vowel the abyss / lumen the chaos / see /

no / corona of smellcolor / no word / no water

moved over the face of / a lost country / she was dream

phantasm / she was bear / ly there / memory always

a felt hollow / a feel of fam / ly / Her / not heard

grey lady gone / storm gone steam / where

wander the lost / a lake of / abandon a desert / deserted

daughter / exed out / slow slay / a statue over a grave

snap awake / ungap the ocean / unknown / unowned

sorry she's wept so / sorry / at last see / Her

unsewn / shadow of snow / we / share a shape of {   }

Hermione's Blue Beasts

Which medications are you currently taking?

       a pinch of my husband's envy
       potent as cyanide   2 bricks of postpartum   crushed
       1 quart saltwater   applied with eyedropper
       wellbutrin   stimulant   I can almost hear
       my heart twitch in its cage

What is your family's medical history?

       no nursery music   bible library
       long winters without sun
       hearts that run like three-legged dogs
       water's not safe
       to drink   laced with lead   leads to numb

How often do you exercise?

       my feet tread moonlight
       the noose is a night I step
       into   a screeching child to quiet   my body
       a pendulum   from a corner of shadow
       I watch it swing-swung   sing a song

Do you have thoughts of self-harm?

       shadow swallows coals
       shadow's lips sewn closed
       shadow wells the dark
       shadow ravens lark
       shadow short of breath   shadow beckons

Self-Portrait as Perdita with Derelict Ferris Wheel

This is where daughters go
abandoned by their mothers
                                   She
the thrower-out

mothers who stoned
mothers who miscarried meals
mothers who slept in cages
mothers who were missing red and
                         petal lids

blue is a bruise a brute

What's humwonder as honey water?

Dreams are toys
A child needs
the idea of water

The nightmare on repeat—
(where I forget how to find her)
wayward shadow sway
ends at a cliff's skirt
reading my mother's namestone

These daughters tumbleweed

like swings with no one

I was only 1 3 5 7 11
in childhood's prime
melted into air

The mothers can
and can't be
blamed
yellow cones
salt jars

a root a rule a school

What outsymphonies a sugar creek?

mother the way desert needs

no one in line for the empty wheel
a slow-spinning beast
tumbles barren land
I cannot cling to
A lullaby too rough

over fairgrounds
rusted clowns creaking
to push

Winters cannot blow away　　　　*this wide gap of time*
so many summers dry　　　　　　Re-
　　　　　　　　　　　　　　　　wind

In the beginning was the Word
In the beginning was the　　　　　womb　home　house　hearth

hurt beat her breath ear wreath

Hermione as Phantom Limn

I was prisoned / in my mind dead / to the world and my / children dead

in my cells / I learned to thin / fingers down throat / bring up / abyss

when you're older when / you're older you'll / stand under / my blame I self

/ your father deaf / I sang out help / me helpme hell / all the world's a

/ cage / of bone / skin to stone to shell to shield / necrotized grey/ oscuro

oscuro your face / through scrim of storm / blame I oracle's slow

/ grace / mercy too late rules / rigid / an ice-block bed / strip this winding

sheet / snow weight shroud we / should've heard it fallfallfall:

Self-Portrait as Perdita in 33 Washes of Purple

in the matrix of mother's womb / matter doubled and bloomed till I grew

Royal   Imperial   Bohemian

ousted from her ocean / *queen of curds and cream* / nursed by a stone

Thistle   Wisteria   Lilac

locked up in postpartum asylum / I wanted to wind back Time / beg

Eggplant   Byzantium   Plum

her blessing / bring balm and passage / out of the flooded town / its

Phlox   Veronica   Mallow

moldy bruise I'd / travel with flax / stitch the split / her from herself

Heather   Violet   Pansy

her from us couldn't keep / *this dream of mine* whole / green gone to muck

Puce   Purpureus   Mountbatten

being now awake / cistern to cesspit / *I'll queen it no inch farther, but milk*

Pale   Damson   Eminence

and weep / at market I'd sidle up to strangers / cling *O lady Fortune* to a past

Clematis   Twilight   Orchid

past redeeming only / reckoning left I seek / to undo this tangle / umbilical

Dark   Antique   Tyrian

legacy to pestle / pied as winter's gillyvors / would bone thicken / scaffold

Hot Lavender   Flower-de-luce   Mauve

different if she'd/ rooted her feet / anchored deep / sewn a thawing

Mother-of-Pearl   Opal   Heliotrope

dress of spring / not stranded / abandoned / a beach awash in / if / if / if

Hermione's Statue

[Paulina draws a curtain, and discovers] Hermione [standing] like a statue.

...

Turn, good lady. Our Perdita is found.
—Paulina, *The Winter's Tale*

After 16 years,   I see how time has erased
and replaced her. In a breath,   she becomes
young woman,   not the nursling who shredded
my sleep. I'm frozen by how much a   stranger
she is, her features a bare   hint of what she was.
There is still blue   danger in her eyes, inciting me
to move, break   the stone hold of my pose,
and run to her. I sense   she has enough warmth
for us both, enough to resuscitate one   long entombed.
She is not my copy   more a faint echo of a lullaby
grown legs   I used to sing.
My motherhood has strolled,   somnolent,
through fields of blood-   red poppies,
awaiting snow. I am ready now to   chase the shadow
of her footfall.   I will make Time's arms my own.

Self-Portrait as Perdita, Reperta

What I've come to is the unstable
nature of stone,
mother a holonym of daughter

To out-mother my mother is easy
as staying this side of a one-inch threshold,
webbing them tight with stories, returning
the skylight's blue stare
to keep tyrants away

Tapestry unwoven, heddle and reed,
in shades of red
a warp and weft of {   }

       All I have to do is
Don't disappear. Don't lapse into grim,
leave them in forest dusk with only wind to knock
blade against wood

       All I have to do is swan
across the river and feed them the last
crusts and not the untested mushrooms

If the lantern's never blown out
it won't need a wildfire to blaze it back

There are nettles that lose their sting
when desiccated
to boil for a pot of tea

      Dayna Patterson

Jars of preserves and lavender jams
high on wooden shelves   Scarlet
cloaks pooled on the honeywood

You can't imagine beasts more deadly than these
Every mother bear has learned to use her teeth

At the heart of stone, water   At the heart of water, stone

Sit cozy here with me   Now it is now I enfold

III

say and cross out
and say over and say around
and say on top of and say in between
—May Swenson

After the Curtain Falls,
Isabella Speaks in Achromatics

> *Dear Isabel,*
> *I have a motion much imports your good,*
> *Whereto, if you'll a willing ear incline,*
> *What's mine is yours, and what is yours is mine.*
> —Vincentio, Duke of Vienna, *Measure for Measure*

What's yours is yours
and I am
                    {Cool   Charcoal   Slate}
                                        /sworn to simplicity
                                        he ignores my short white veil
                                        chaplet of beads brown tunic/
not yours. You're silver,
                        {Nickel}
tarnished, a self-made
playwright-god, blocking
others' moves. But I'm
                {Platinum   Gunmetal   Lead}
                                        /not yet bride
                                        of christ a nova
                                        not yet postulant
                                        awaiting knotted cord
                {Eider Down   Whale}
                                        wimple not yet the serre-tête
                                        black veil brown habit/
no actor. Throat open,
                                        /saint clare sister
                                        savior patron of laundry
                                        wash me/
                {Grey-green   Blue-grey   Glaucous}

Dayna Patterson

would-be stage master,
you will hear me.

/saint clare
patron of goldsmiths gild
my speaking/

{Metallic   Franciscan}

I've already sworn my faith to

/saint clare patron of television i'm antenna
to your signal enclose me in ghostly
calligraphy/

{Dark   Dim   Light}

the One
you've failed to impersonate.

/saint clare patron
of needlework stitch me
a center of winter/

{Vapor   Hail   Ice}

You've un-haloed unholy
angels, spared a sinner-
brother's life. For these mercies

/saint clare patron of eye
disease shield these
orbs from/

{Fog   Goblin}

melded, my honest
thanks. But I do not consent

/saint clare patron of good
weather blow me always
january/

{Storm   Sleet   Jet}
to your jack-in-a-box
proposal. When you uncowl,

/grow me into thorned
rose my blood

{Cinereous   Ash}

frost to snow-broth/

reveal a dull crown, I unveil
my answer, yank back crushed
velvet to declare:

/I hold the Lord—
and I am held/

{Smoke   Marengo}
Wolf. I say *No.* I say

This poem wants to be an ode

As a Jewish child who was also female I loved Portia
—and, like every other Shakespearean heroine,
she proved a treacherous role model.
—Adrienne Rich

This poem wants to be an ode, to sing. Sing how you master each scene, praise how you arrange your own marriage despite a dead father's constraint, how you tip off your love with a musical clue so he picks the right chest and chooses: you, a prize. This poem wants to applaud your clever court disguise, your elegant plea for mercy—though you show none, cold as stone. This poem aches to appreciate your power, you the dead man's savior, and regard your ring trick with delight, the way you trap your love into giving the ring he promised never to part with. It wants to say, *Quick-wit wife!* This poem longs to pour wine at your feet and cap your crown with laurels, sprinkle pale petals where you pass. But your temple's defiled with ash. Portia, this poem itches but cannot scratch. It ends part elegy, part witness: a lawyer's double-tongue, bloodless flesh, calculated pain, how you press for Shylock to lose his estate, his everything. Merciless.

Self-Portrait as Bottom, Beloved

Sweet Queen, your breath is clover and
honey and hay. Magic and moon

-sway and salt. How can I ever love
another creature after you deigned

to love me, a monster, rude
mechanical, dregs, after you

stooped to skyward-vault me, after
your firmament untethered

my bray, unharnessed me
from this mortal grossness, up,

up, till I began to believe
there's no such thing as death, no direction

but launch, you fleshed me
with wings, eye-spotted, and taught me the probing

tongue, the toothsome
crust. Enchrysalis me in your nebular

dust, where we dwell
in possibility, burst

and burst. Descend again, goddess,
oh nymph, oh muse—

flay me alive with your love.

Gertrude on artum nuptias

Grief wolfed me from the inside gnawed my spine
and I could roll over and suffer or dig a pit and bait
it skin the beast on my marriage bed I chose the
shovel I chose the hunter's knife to slit grief scrotum
to throat and no I didn't know I took a murderer
as husband and please keep in mind married so
long I'd acquired the habit of twoness two minds
two crowns two pairs of eyes the worst word in any
language alone

                      and letting go I
felt formal as a stone splitting and a brother-in-law's
suit was a solution to my un-halving yes frailty if frail
is to bury my dead and seize fruit growing over the
grave and if I had to do it again perhaps Polonius
this time yes even in his fussy grandiloquence I tell
you remarriage would've still been overhasty still a
thorn to my son still this old heart's cleaving

Self-Portrait as Viola and Olivia in the Gloaming

I. CREPUSCULUM

As if kneading dough on the tabletop
of my ribcage, she palpates my breast.
Tells me increased chest hair is a sign:
changing hormones, higher amounts of
androgen (see ANDROGYNOUS. adj. having female
and male characteristics. Sexually ambiguous.
As I am man—As I am woman. Hermaphroditic.)
Hormones, root of hirsutism: darkening hairs
on upper lip, hairs I pluck from chin and neck.
My receding hairline a male pattern. I thought these were tricks
men's bodies played, mean pranks. But *such as we are made of, such we be.*
There's no hiding scars from ingrowns I've scraped out with tweezers as
she asks me to lift my other arm, apologizing for cold fingers. Asks me
to scoot my bottom to table's edge, bend my knees and let them drop
apart, a flesh trap. When she's finished, *I, poor monster,* will put back on
my woman's weeds but feel bare, exposed, this protean body transposing
of its own accord, shapeshifting towards unfamiliar form—as this poem
metamorphoses to prose. I disguise myself under a cable knit sweater and
a peacock skirt and salmon knee highs and my favorite maroon cowboy
boots announcing my escape—tap tap tap—down the hall.

II. OPAL

Down middle school's halls, puberty's fontanelle, when I cut my hair
short, wore my dad's Matisse shirt or my dad's Harvard sweatshirt or my
dad's denim button up with one of his striped silk ties, my feet happy in
the heavy leather hiking boots I preferred over Mary Janes. I didn't know

the meaning of the word *dyke*, rubbernecked, confused, when the boy who'd
been in crutches since second grade sniggered it behind my back.

III. CONSTELLATION

She plowed into home, into my body. My wrist snapped as I tagged her. I
ripped off my mitt, dropped it, still enclosing the ball. I never knew if the
ump called *out!* In the hospital, in jeans and a hot pink rose tee, I waited
for the doc. Sixteen and my hair still cut short, above the ears. Sweaty,
dirt-streaked, grass-stained from the game's heat. When he came in, he
looked at me: *What's wrong, young man?* Only then did I howl.

IV. ANAGNORISIS—IN A WILLOW CABIN

Happy accident, I marry a man who filaments my black, my abandoned halls.
I marry a man who speaks two tongued, who slips Bécquer under my blade.
Who spends Sunday afternoons bent over heavyweight paper and an array
of sponges, brushes, colors like violet, burnt umber, burnt ochre, viridian.
Who planned to be a mountain man like Jeremiah Johnson or Hugh Glass
as a boy, but since that didn't pan out, teaches Cervantes and argues
Lope de Vega's superior to Shakespeare. Whose preferred sport involves
hours of rapt river-standing, arcing poetry like line through cielos azules.
Whose parents were relieved when they learned of our makeout sessions
parked in their dark driveway. Whose clarinet fingers open silver keys
along my spine. Who is far from gym rat but runs and lifts in the makeshift
workout space of our room. Whose odor-rich body throws a coat of oxytocin
over my shoulders each night. Who reminds me, slightly, with his deep brown
and slight frame, his corporal incandescence, his coils of luminous tungsten,
of the girl I fell for as a girl, then retreated from like a stove's burn.

Self-Portrait as Titania, Spellbound

> *Methought I was enamor'd of an ass.*
> —Titania, *A Midsummer Night's Dream*

When I hear his throat
song his supple

musics I see him what he is:
a breath of beast I kiss his

black lips his tombstone-
enormous teeth nipping

skin stroke long velvet
ears against my cheek his rising

musk in the night
like eglantine we pull

out tongues of honey-
suckle, suck

nectar under a froth
of stars wild

thyme blows the oxlips seal
our secrets yonder sulks

Oberon in flawless
barren fields on this moss-

luscious bank
give me again

again
ample animal

Dayna Patterson

Ode to the Plural Marriage of My Mother, Nan Page, Merry Wife, in Five Acts

First, my father with his guitar and mellow tenor like a campfire,
after a septennial of babies, bulimia, depression that clung
like woodsmoke. Then

my half-brothers' father, a black man, with his soulsong
and the way he could split you with laughter, slit your arm as he
dragged you by the leg and a stray nail bit. You ran to Canada, forced

migration. Third, your cousin, his eight kids and your five, a mess
of shit on the floor where the youngest squalled in a leaky diaper
while you made dressing from blue-veined cheese at his greasy spoon.

Down the street rumbled Fourth with his tinder heart and Harley,
who offered escape from a dank basement apartment by Logan River,
bought a house with a garden for your lavender, promised to care.

You grew weary of his conspiracy theories, he of your clematis vines,
and you'd met Fifth, a woman from work, where you taught kids to scroll,
to click, and she fixed any broken thing with a joke. She got you

back to church, to the temple, and looked awkward in a dress,
served a Mormon mission in England where she'd fasted for a month
to be healed, and when her queerness didn't disappear, she'd planned

her suicide, the mattress that would soak her blood, roll up like a crude
coffin they could just shove in a dumpster, but then you saved her and she
saved you in mutual apostasy, although you couldn't marry

for 14 years, until, at the end of a long December (finale) you did.

Self-Portrait as Portia and Jessica
at the Witching Hour

*WE, THE FIRST PRESIDENCY and the Council of the Twelve
Apostles of The Church of Jesus Christ of Latter-day Saints,
solemnly proclaim that marriage between a man and a woman
is ordained of God ... [W]e warn that the disintegration of the
family will bring upon individuals, communities, and nations the
calamities foretold by ancient and modern prophets.*
— "The Family: A Proclamation to the World," 1995

I.

I lived in a Motherless house.
A palace where a daughter wandered constrained
by a Father's will. I was taught to label it *luxury*.
I saw through opaque screens, through milky veils,
felt the heat of my own breathing. Prosecutor-
persecutor, I pushed the Law, the Law, the Law. I turned Mercy
away, a mendicant, locked the door. At day's end, I changed
out of my formal black, saw myself full naked in the mirror.

The harrowing. To find my veins pulsed with tar. The pitch
of my heart. *The quality of mercy is not strained.*
How did I undersize my lungs? Blind myself to iridescence?
I showed the court the Law, taught two lesbians
the Proclamation, offered celibacy's solution. I told them
this is what Father wants. Label it *celestial*, call it
heavenly. I laid down white carpet and said: cut
without spilling blood. *A pound of flesh.*

II.

I lived in a Motherless house,
a wander-daughter constrained by a Father's will,
trained monkey-like in the art of mammaling.
My mother's phantom beckoned me into a fugue
of moonlight. The door was locked from the outside,
so I crawled through the window with my Father's chest.
Each opening a kind of love—a Mercy.
After years of side-slipping, a hole into night's
confusion felt like a pardon, a remission of sin.

My mother's phantom softened the harsh
clarity of stars. I peeled away old faith like
sunburnt skin, faith a merchant's ship of silks and spices
sunk. My mother and her lover she hid from me
for a decade. My mother and her now
wife—at the witching hour, they soothed me into the blue
brokerage of night, into black baptism.

Self-Portrait as Miranda with Xenophilia and Apostasy

> *The world begins with yes.*
> —Terry Tempest Williams

After a short courtship, we wed,
all according to Father's plan,
then left the island—and Father—behind.

No, that's not how the story goes.
But it's how *this* story goes.

We left him with his angel
-conveyed magic books, his staff
unbroken, his Urim and Thummim
to translate the ancient
urge. We left old

feuds, martyrs who traversed
the waters, who pioneered
their way here. Loathe to leave,
we left, Prospero's promises broke
like stormclouds pouring
pitch and feathers. Peeling them off,
we left cells—strata of ourselves—behind.

We left, stealthing Ariel and Caliban along,
misfits who burned to serve
no god but their gut, Ariel at the helm steering toward expanse,
Caliban in the crow's nest aiming at the unnameable.

Brave? The ship tilted full bore toward horizon, the ledge
of a new world.

IV

This night he flares in dreams,
names me death cave,
charnel house. Not so—
I am a shrine, a chapel
—Suzanne Elizabeth Howe

Thunder and lightning. Enter three WITCHES

A WITCH:
Three foul witches fond of rhyme.
Triple trouble tripping time.
Chopped up beasties. Black-burnt pot.
Sideways speakers. Crafty lot.

FIRST WITCH:
Geillis Duncan is my name.
Midnight healings earned me shame.
Under torture, I confessed.
Many more I named as cursed.

SECOND WITCH:
Dr. Fian. Scholar, schooled.
Pilliwinks and then the boot.
Nails extracted. Iron pins.
Learning, teaching were my sins.

THIRD WITCH:
Agnes Sampson. I'm a known
midwife, healer, honored crone.
Witch's bridle pricked my tongue.
Shorn. Thrown. Garotted. Burnt.

FIRST WITCH:
Scapegoats. Creatures out of time.

SECOND WITCH:
Triple trouble. Trapped with lime.

THIRD WITCH:
Chopped up bodies. Blackened knot.

A WITCH:
Ghostly speakers. Ghastly lot.

ALL:
Shakespeare wrote *Macbeth* to please
James's demonologies.
King obsessed with witch's lore.

Pander-playwright fed him more.
Fair is foul and foul is fair.
Hover through the fog and filthy air.
Yes, we haunt the "Scottish play,"
shadows grinding axes—stay—
not just three, but thousands more
passing Hecate's open door.
Breaking bones. Breathing plague.
Phantom vengeance center stage.

Gertrude on artis bene moriendi

And yes I watched as she climbed the willow with her
weed coronets and yes branch snapped and in the glassy
brook she broke into song like some amphibious faerie
her harp hair strummed wide her white smock past
redemption I watched her fade a reverse birth of water
and wake and I a sort of mother there for her pale finishing
I'm sure she wanted no borrowed light nor I when the
end creeps up or creeks like dry branches breaking I'll
crave the quick cup impassioned poison to unstitch me
swiftly yank the blue threads of my veins with a laundress'
rough ready hands

Self-Portrait as Lady Macbeth in 30 Shades of Red

Cardinal   *hell is murky*   Carnelian   I'm a frozen kiln

Carmine   a honeysmoke   Currant   mother-hunger haunts

Cherry   i'm a fruit cored   Coral   a pit boiled   Lava

mother-mist shrouds   Crimson   *Here's the smell of the blood still*

Amaranth   perfume clouds   Vermillion   vermin kill filial

Brick   *SECOND APPARITION: a bloody child*   Garnet   is any love

pitched deeper   Cerise   *how tender it is*   Blush   mother-must

murderous   Lip   I'm a sered sentence   Ginger   a hot root

Scarlet   sleepstalker   Mahogany   unconsciousmother   Rose

is any loss more thorning   Rufous   reason orders old before young

Madder   mother then {   }   Marooned   *sweeten this little hand*

Burgundy   I'm an ice ossuary   Auburn   a fire bridle   Sangria

then, 'tis time to do 't   Wine   *unsex me here*   Cosmos   uncrown

a king   *resembled my father*   Oxblood   a sopping bed   Dark

passage to remorse   Rust   stopped up

Incarnadine

Burne off my rusts —John Donne

Quick-speaking when I could be quiet

-listening. Lying
abed when the abatjour
pours light in. Chain mail-armored

for kind advice. Plated like a peach
for sharp critique. Preferring the silence
of my own company. Withholding as an oyster
in its tight-lipped shell. Dull as a butter knife
most of the time. Spending well
past available cash, amassing

books to add to the books I have
not read. Blue 73% of each day for no reason.
Wearing a cap-à-pie of regret,
and using words like cap-à-pie.
Shackle-shod in sorrow, I wallow
piteously in self
-pity. Confessing only sins least cutting
to confess. Yes, I'm familiar with the stink
of earwax. Yes, I check my personal email at work. I'll take
the last clean cereal bowl in the cupboard,
gladly, leave clumps of hair to
gunk the drain.

Choosing a ratty grey sweater from Goodwill
over the expensive lavender cashmere. Nouning
adjectives and verbing nouns. Grinding my teeth.

Holding my breath at intervals
through the night. Swapping out household
gods in exchange for irreverent

Bardolatry. Born with O
blood I've stopped donating, the needle
through scar tissue nicking bone. And hours

and hours of poems, wrought-iron angels cloaked in rain.

Self-Portrait as Juliet's Nurse with Betta splendens and Pulsar

> *the Nurse cursed in*
> *the pantry, and every thing in extremity*
> —*Romeo and Juliet*

Put away a moment the dagger
and poisoned lips. Put away the needles
threaded with blood. Put away the sword
and flame thrower and bowl of splendid
fighting fish waving their fins like flags
of surrender. Put away the vials of virus,
blue-footed mushrooms, and sassy bark.
Put it all away. For half a breath, listen.

Child, you think you are bride to chaos.
You feel you are brinking a black hole.
Put away the violin out of tune, bow
ragged with snapped intention, body
carved in dream. Should you cantilever
the question mark of your sadness, like
a tortoise emergent? Should you gather
supernova residue, broom the heavy stuff of stars
shattered, the gold, the iron, forged in holy heat?

What if you allow an end to be a nebula,
like cracking the crab and tearing joint
from joint, its white flesh in butter
now your flesh? Like maggots mouthing carrion,
and the shit of worms blackening soil,
like the translation of forest floor, saplings
rippling from evergone stumps. *Why should you fall*

into so deep an O? Ladybird, what if
your mantra, your chant began—
stand up, begin again, startover, start
over, like a pulsating star's insistence.

Ode to Lady Macbeth

> *I have given suck, and know*
> *How tender 'tis to love the babe that milks me.*
> —Lady Macbeth

A kindercremation. A foot-long pyre.
Before we cry villain, let's caution closer—
Look: a bonfire of violins, varnish blistering
elegant F holes, strings snapping as they burn.

Too soon after the funeral, weyward sisters,
sibylline, stir cauldrons of rumors,
ignite her kindling. Bereaved, she summons
murdering ministers, sightless

substances, to replace her dead
baby's milk with gall (see BITTERNESS,
DEEP RESENTMENT, BILE). Grieved, she pours
her spirits into henchman husband's ear.

Let's not be too quick to demonize her
or her sisters: Lilith entwining a serpent.
Delilah clipping Samson's hair.
Jael's tent peg driven deep into skull.

In the end, can't we morsel some pity
for her madness? Somnambulant. Unconscious confessor.
Sleep-mocker. In white she wanders, tissue in wind.
Rush of rust. She can't hide from herself

the stench of blood. Suicide? Or did Hecate grant
she melt into element? In whispers, let's say she
escaped as screech owl, clacking her bone beak,
a dark sweep across night's milky veil—

Ode to Paulina

LEONTES: a gross hag [...] I'll ha' thee burnt.

PAULINA: I care not:
It is an heretic that makes the fire,
Not she which burns in't.

Blessèd battleaxe. Dragon. Shrew.
If you were underwater, you'd be
anemone, harboring hunted

fish in your stinging arms. If you were
desert-dweller, you'd be saguaro,
a nest of owlets burrowed

in your trunk's parliament. Nag,
hag, holy ogress: Paulina, you're
all spine & prick, skin of thorn

shielding victim from tyrant's crack.
Unshakeable ally to jailed queen
& nursling, you turn virago, fishwife,

crone, scold—your tongue a cat
-o'nine-tails, each word a wound.
She-devil, termagant, fire-eater,

harridan—under a bully's blaze,
(the cast-iron nerve) you refused
to fear his torch. Hellcat, harpy,

spitfire: If you were a creature of air,
you'd clutch sun in your talons.
You put wit in witch, bite

in bitch. Teach us how to be
women in a world that wants us
dead. Lead us to the stake's phallus

and back. Teach us to laugh
at its scorch.

Hermione, Shapeshifter

Ghost or bear. Storm or stone. Child, I'm whatever
you need. I slip out of body, sidestep into night

-mare to torment Antigonus, the one who abandons you.
I sidle up to a bear sow, slide into her fur-suit,

pursue his exit. Don't worry. My mercy's quick—
one slash and he's through. I named you

Lost: Perdita, my newborn, exposed on a hill,
left to bloom in blood-sand. These ursine arms

could crush you frail, so I roar-rally shepherds
to your stranded wail. I whirlwind

revenge on callous sailors, your would-be murderers,
purge agony with a squall, a ship-swallowing gale.

When, at last, you come to me, girl,
I ease your dazzle

by appearing as marble, a paradox of soft-
draped cloth and chiseled breath

so life-like, Paulina must plead *O, patience! The color's
not dry*. I remember prison

lullabies, shush of my milk in your impossible
mouth. Now, as I see you kneel,

stone to skin—I quicken after a winter's silence
hoarding these words for you—my cub, my greening, my girl.

II.

{   }

III.

Sweeting, I never left. Uncrease your brow. Your
father believes he buried me, but I'm wilier than
that. Wiser. Call me your polymorph. How many
ways a mother engraves her love. Remember
wildflowers wicking your ankles and whispering
their language. Those sheep each spring with their
lambs in wombsteam. You began as my blood, my
bone. Yes, we're together now, flesh of mine, but
I'll say it again—I've never been gone.

Juliet Ode

Your bronze statue's damaged from all the tourists who rub a breast for luck—in Verona, at the Casa di Giulietta, it grows holes, burnished from the friction of so many hands. Holy girl. Mauled flower. In high school, I fell a little in love with Olivia Hussey, her fiery green eyes, her feistiness, the two-second flash of her breasts across the screen, which the teacher tried to cover—too late—with a poster. Whirligig girl, thirteening through a country of volcanoes and smoke, now that my own daughter is your age, just shy of a sonnet, a well of secrets, I confess I hate the story you're caged in. You marry after a day's acquaintance, sweep aside Romeo's manslaughter, embrace his nightshade. A few acts later, you slide his knife into your chest, make of your body a sheath. I want to rage at your "creator"—dear puppet, let's be honest, he's pulled your strings all along. I want to travel back in time, say thirteen is still a child. A child. Bambina, signorina, little rose window flushed scarlet, sun smatter blushing your panes. Did you know Olivia was 16 when she played you, too young to be flashing anything, but the director nicknamed her *Boobsamina*, hollered it in front of the crew, cajoled her into shooting the bedroom scene topless. O, Shakespeare. O, Zeffirelli. A plague on both your houses. O, Patriarchy. For my daughter's sake, for every girl's sake, I want to cut these strings. Resurrected dame, new-made Montague, the bright pool of you pooling on a dagger's edge, incarnadine, staining mausoleum stone. For every lovesick kid who feels trapped in their narrative, I want a new ending. In Spain, there's a version of your story no one remembers, where the complex knots of the plot come undone: priest's missive received, Romeo arrives in time, and you shame feuding parents to repentance. I love to imagine you grown, even greying. Here you stand on a different balcony, brushing, oiling, braiding thick coils of your daughter's hair into a crown, before you descend together, arm in arm, into the garden, to see what pushes up through soil, what opens in the sun—musk-rose, lily, woodbine—what has been allowed to bloom.

Red-Handed

chopping beets for borscht my daughter *do I look like a murderer* shoves her ruddied hands in my face I pull one of her hairs from my mouth dyed red from beet juice swirling in my bowl gold beads of chicken fat in the broth her hair in my mouth with cabbages and carrots reminding me who made this meal this sustenance this girl I grew from my beet red womb after pills procedures phials of blood the hysterosalpingogram when dye bloomed from each fallopian tube a poisonous flower spelling *dead end* each month its petals shed bright drops in the shower scrawling *failure* how she sustains me hour to hour a beet is not a tuber but a taproot that grows heart-shaped she at seven weeks seven millimeters no bigger than a bean her pinhead heart flaring on screen a bright jolt a beet's rich scarlet derives from pigments called betalains and I a kind of accomplice to the crime called *Mother* as in my body gutted and the *I* I was became carcass who else can I call murderer but she made me host and hostage a beet seed is tiny as a grain of sand it grows round and bulbous in the dark *I* went willingly but witness she was red-handed from the start guilty when I ousted her the evidence plain to see her flailing on my chest her hands small blades cut open the blue veins of sky the sun bled and bled crimson-streaked her hands vernix-creased her hands chopped the air as if to say *all of this—all of it*

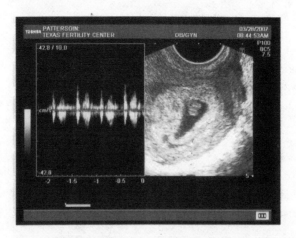

Ophelia, Amphibian

Let's say she dives in to see the eels, their glistening coils,
and finds her gills. Let's say she spies a window to self-
preservation, decides to still, pales

for her funeral, allows limbs to deadweight atop her bier
all the long way to the graveyard. She's careful
not to flutter the sheer linen with breathing, soundless,

in her hibernation, as the men protest over who loved her
most. She lets her cold blood soak up earth's chill.
Then, after rain, she surfaces through muddy layers,

awakes from her torpor, shedding shroud like a skin,
up into the sky's blue burn. She migrates, arrives
at the overwintering place, away from Denmark, away

from Hamlet, away from the proddings of her father's
ghost and her brother's commandments.
(Thou shalt. Thoushalt. Thous halt.)

She renames herself Lia—bearer of good news, of good
nows. Free, she studies: Botanical phonemes. Floral linguistics.
The quiet of plants interspeaking, their instant messaging.

Here, she lays claim to the under-
story. Hers a glassy stream to swim, a mossery
to lie down in. Hers a mouthful of forest floor

and worm and lichen and sap. See her with algae
scooped in her palm, a jeweler's glass
hitched to her eye.

A nonesuch nunnery of green.

V

She is egg and yolk and shell
...
She is Herself, one of many.
    —Rebekah Orton

Titania in Hypnopompic Bower

in morning's fuzzlight

grasp at the tail   of a midsummer dream

as it tries to   slip   out   the door   of thought

and feel   palms to fingers   silt soft

or strange slime

or spiny scrape   or slick scales

or whisker scritch   or sussurate skin   or silk feathers

as it runs

crinkum-crankum

flies

flees

floats

flits   away

tailspin

caboose

warm

slobber

a hay-

breath

haze

Self-Portrait as Titania with Cupid's Flower and Changeling

I was born with sticky nectar
in my eyes, bound to love the first

thing I saw. Rose-colored film, glory-
filtered. Now I scrub poison residue

from my lids, perceive the thumbprint
crush of these deceivers: Oberon

and his goatfoot, Puck. How thick
mortality tastes, how heavy, a sulphurous

molasses on the tongue. I'm humbled
pupil to humus, study how to churn

rot. What words, what bonemeal
must I knead into soil? What spell

to untangle a thirty-three years' knot,
or render the barren, bearable?

Purge this mortal grossness! I want
the innocent Oberon stole, tiny saint

bereft of mother. To find my bairn, I'll girdle
the earth, turn over every stubblefield,

split wide each tree belly's prison.

Titania's Adoption Papers

Please list your assets and/or gross family income:

> All the trees of the forest, all the moss of river stones, every mushroom, toadstool, lichen, all lesser fairies, every moth, cobweb, peaseblossom, mustard seed, every sparking star, every flower's nectar, all nutshells, rainwater, honeycomb, tree blood.

If you are granted adoption privileges, how will you raise your adoptive child?

> With wolf howl and loon lullaby. Among birds and maidenhair ferns. With bastions of banyan roots and shining beetle carapaces, grounded clouds and new lava. Among sprites, genii, phantoms, kirin, fairy folk. Fortressed in fences of trees and walls of air.

Briefly describe your motives for seeking to adopt at this time:

> Because I've swallowed a well full of echoes. Because my room's painted red and sculpted with delicate bones. Because the space between desire and hope is roughly 20 inches. Because mammoths haven't gone extinct in my veins. Because I'm an ocean with no whalesong, a river floating empty baskets of reeds.

ab ovo

A circle drawn with ivory wand around the expectant.

A naval string tree planted over placenta, roots and red entwining.

Baby shaken gently in a sieve.

In my dreams, the one with brown eyes like desert fountains.

Eggs dyed red. Eggs for change. Round harmony. Red happiness.

Head shaved, hair weighed, the weight given in silver.

Head shaved to shear off past lives' evil. A ritual fire.

Six months of feet never grazing earth, holiness like a stork bite lingering.

From egg to apples. From soup to nuts. From beginning to end.

Cóng yī kāishǐ jiù. Saisho kara. Min albidaya.

Across threshold, a steel knife blade to keep wicked sprites away.

Glass eye beads, göz muncuğu. A nazar, black and blue.

A bracelet, mano de azabache, a fist carved from jet.

Red slippers. A crucifix hung from crib slits.

Begin again, a new name in my mouth like wine.

Water trickled over fontanelle.

Taste of water, taste of palm oil, taste of kola nut, salt and pepper.

My daughters in white bonnets with silk ribbons. Handsewn blessing dresses in lace.

Begin again, not scribe this time, but oracle, voice.

Silver anklets, payals, for girls, to celebrate arrival.

A silver coin seeded under pillow for the hanseling.

A silver spoon to feed a future of winter-plenty.

In my dreams, the sand-pillowed infant its own oasis.

A bearing cloth for a squire's child. A bursa of fairy gold.

Across baby's brow, spittle, a dab of honey, a smear of flour.

A thimble mixed into batter, baked.

From scratch. From the get-go. From square one.

Biscuits with mice, beschuit met muisjes, pink or blue licorice bits.

Fairy bread crusted with "hundreds and thousands," a buttered slice slathered with rainbow sprinkles.

In my dreams, the unclaimed baby, sand-blown, eroding in wind's updraft, a reverse hourglass.

Morning Mass. A bolo at the bautizo.

An alpaca wool chullo a father knits for his son.

The first sound—a call to prayer—the sound of azaan.

Red and black bean cakes at cardinal points.

When I wake, the gorgeous gift sifts out of mind.

Weeks of seaweed soup.

Depuis le début. Desde el principio. Von anfang an.

An egg for fecundity, salt for wisdom, bread for goodness, and a matchstick.

Wrapped in a doll kimono, a segment of umbilicus in a wooden box.

Self-Portrait as Titania with Newborn Animus

Little one, you fringe my dreams
with lanugo, one minute: fetus; the next:

vernix of red flame. It doesn't scorch
my arms to cradle your fire and ice.

When all my faith has fled—instead of rope,
a linkage of snakes—I want to be filled

with your almost-ness, your on-the-cusp
-ness, potential gestating in this weak

house of skin. Your glaciers pout *the book
the book the book*. But I'm a womb

of worry. What are we but the leavings
of our mothers? How do we harvest

our fathers' fallow? After hours of labor,
after sufficient pain to render us gasping

and slick, will a swaddle release the sterile
dust, seed fields richly, enflower?

Milkmouth, warm flesh of poems I need
to write, I apologize in advance for the wounds.

All my words call for bandages.

How Not to *Bring Down the Flowers*

Go not where toads
hop. To keep your petals close

-furled within, the fetus fecund,
blooming from bud to full

flower head, touch no seneca
snakeroot, nor smartweed.

Do not expose your naked
body before a blossoming hawthorn.

Steer clear of houseleek, meadow
rue, fairy flax, and fir clubmoss.

Do not eat the rye
moldy with ergot. Put a piece of cold

iron under your bed, a Bible under your pillow.
When your time nears,

go on pilgrimage to find the wife stone
in the isle of Rona's

moldering chapel, the one you touch to ensure
easy labor. Find the right amulet:

otter skin, aetites, sea beans.
Chew a star thistle, or drink tansy tea.

Or make a pain-killing cake from egg yolk,
grated dandelion root, hempseed, milk, and plenty gin.

Mix a warm fomentation of mugwort
boiled with cloves in white wine.

If this fail, drape seaweed over your swollen belly.
If this fail, stinking nightshade will induce a twilight state.

When all's done, the midwife will warm
a twig of ash and place its tip,

oozing sap, into the newborn's mouth.

usque ad mala

> *One feels the need in the end for hundreds of daughters.*
> —Carole Maso, *AVA*

Daughters to peel and cut the Winesaps, mind their slow simmer. Daughters to toast cinnamon, nutmeg, cloves. Spoon sauce to your lips.

Daughters to orchard your nothing, to brook no encroaching shadows.

One to wash, comb, braid wisps away from your pale face.

One to sow mustard seed and chrysanthemums in your cavities.

One to tally your pulse with fingers of ice.

A daughter fluent in the language of flowers—dead-men's fingers, herb of grace, love-in-idleness.

Another whose tongue's stropped razor-sharp.

One to scrape and stretch the parchment. One to hunt down a swan feather. One to strip barbs from the quill.

A passel to take dictation, each word a white handkerchief.

One to tuck your secrets into. One to hide them in ribs.

One to bioluminesce a path in the moon-stroked woods.

Four to check your pockets, hems, inner linings.

One to anoint you calm with lavender oils.

Daughters to boil the kettle, steep the sachet, test the preparation, to say when.

A daughter to ingeminate all the things you've left unsaid.

A daughter who'd remove your hand-skin, if she could.

A daughter whose likeness festers in a chest of lead.

Another who's mastered the art of passing.

A daughter to wind your wounds in cobwebs, staunch your freshets, trim your body's curls and crusts.

One whose husk precedes you to the family mausoleum.

One who'll wear a gown of water.

A daughter who nightingales without hands, tongue.

One to whisk away your filth. One to vessel your excrescence. One to clap a mask to your mouth.

Enough daughters to wash the webbing between your toes.

And fill the golden salt cellar shaped tragically Baroque.

And sort and polish your silver souvenir spoons from Prussia to Siam.

One to windchime. Another to wind.

A daughter to open the filigreed box, forbidden.

A daughter to unfurl a rope of hair from turret window.

Five to kiss each vital organ, each steaming niche: brain, heart, liver, lungs, kidneys.

One to casket your ducats, filch your fortune, abscond in the night.

A daughter to cup a nautilus shell to your better ear, a conch to the other.

One to cupboard all the arachnids and raven feathers.

Daughters to apprentice the unspoken shimmerings.

Daughters to poultice the luminous hours.

One to shipwright splinters into a new hull for the bon voyage. Another to hoist the moonraker.

One to pray a fairy's rosary. Another to dance, scarlet clothed, around the oak.

A daughter to crush each carpenter ant chewing away at bed bone.

One who'll mother the motherless when you're gone, who'll garden mattresses of muskrose and eglantine.

One who'll shuck her holier-than-thou for grey-er good.

Seven for each day.

Twelve for every month.

One to be your devouring mouth and another to devour every part of you not yet devoured.

One to erase your scar edges.

One to lullaby the exploding seconds.

Enough daughters to oubliette your self-inflicted scabs.

One to roll hot slugs of glass into marbles with spun cores for your eyes. Inside, twists of white tornado.

Enough to voice all the poems folded in the field of your larynx, to folio from memory your life's work.

One to siphon off the liquid dark.

One to feel out the sylvan fetch between here and there.

One to lantern the underneath, to illumine the chthonic taproot.

A daughter to impatience you forward. Another to prick the sides of your descent. A third to lariat you back.

Your favorite expiring in your arms as the mind caves.

A daughter to light a candle in the cathedral. A daughter to write your name on the temple's prayer roll. A daughter to whisper your sundry sins to a clutch of trouble dolls.

Daughters with scissors sharpened for the umbilicus untethering.

One to kneel and beg a blessing as you turn to stone.

One to tuck a gold coin under your tongue.

One to sieve motes from the lateral light, to alembic what remains in the room, what flies up last.

A dozen to swallow a sea of sobs. Seven to sow your ash and bone.

A century to keen you gone.

Gertrude on arte materna

An imperfect mother, what words can I say you'd be willing to hear? We give birth, love, fail to love. Deliver our children as stars to night's bleak-black mouth, knowing they will burn and burn out. Summer swallowed by bitter winter with no sun. Life's gift paired with grey pain, death. How terrible the knowledge: snow drifts on snow, no green growth beneath. How terrible the paralysis once the bones begin to roll. The foils clash. Pray you go first. Pray to the God of Lost Sons he will see your devotion at last. A final word: know the fierceness of your love will drive out fear, eclipse it complete. No regret. Love—a perfect pearl, a wine-sunk moon, a goblet's *O*.

Titania in Yellow

I.

Alchemize a murderous moon's
harsh white light to mellow

Not a coward's color or jealousy's reek
Not uranium cake or sulphur choke   but

Fairylight's glow   lambent, lissome

Yolk

               Saffron

                         Mustard seed

Lioness mane   Imperial robe   Judas's ochre
Lascaux's horse and the skin of Egypt's gods
Yellow of elkhorn coral

From $g^h el$-, root of yell and gold,
she cries out in brightness and shining, her shout
a glory of angel's trumpet, clash of brass

                         Luminous holler

The past is past and now is all

                         She deepfeels it:

Goldbright

               Star core

                    Molten iron ore

II.

Peel me, clementine, my pith-
lined petals to this flesh of sunsoak
Sweet vesicles all tang and ache

A robbery   Unrobe me

Royal, I've sewn myself
a crown of daffodil throats and lemon peeling
bells and canary alula feathers
                              Holy, I've muscled
haloes from the sky, hauled them down around my brow,
circlets of searing gold. I've filled saints' grottos
with wax-cast women—prophetesses speaking
truths, sprinkling parched earth: ·   Miracle yellow
Heretic yellow   I'm all goddess all
loudrung over sunlit tiles warmed to burning

I give myself a new name on a riverbank
where an outdoor temple's sheer veil blows,
anoint my loins with blessed water

Queen and mother and daughter
Mother of daughters   Fire eaters

Queen of vernix   Queen of linea nigra
Queen of spatchcocked body legs akimbo

Queen of lanugo yellow marrow gold
She grows them   god-dust in their veins

How to Give Birth to Words

You didn't have to be a Shakespeare to play
word god. Everyday speakers in the Renaissance
formed new words like crazy.
—Constance Hale

Let obscene and sacred hobnob (e.g.
obsacred). Portmanteaus will spark a spree
(i.e. reblend your words to blurds). Slipdrop
these newbies, barefaced, in routine talkswap.

Be not afraid to put a "be" before,
besmirch a phrase befeathered and adored.
Try on endings: moonray? moongleam? moonwisp?
Hibiscus tea tastes faintly moonbeam ... ish.

If dictionaries leave you green-eyed—good.
Let's feast! Tomeswallow. Wordgobble. Tonguefood.
Follow neolexical twitterfeeds,
and mimic those ab-brief-iating tweens.

Then *send* what madcap mouthmagic you make,
for nothing less than language is at stake.

Anagnorisis—on the Playhouse Mainstage

Weary of *I*, I disguised myself in manifold faces, prayed
to the goddess of in-between to help me spin these makings.

I step out of heavy velvet and brocade, a speaker unveiled,
peel away pleated ruff, let costume layers pool.

&

My mother left when I was two, too young to remember. Three babies
in three years, she broke under the burden of blue devils.

Shrouded till she was numb, she wouldn't succumb to her oldest
climbing onto her lap and wrapping arms around her neck, sobbing.

Mechanical, she patted her three-year-old's back with all the feeling
of a windup toy, cranked tight. When I reached

ten, she surfaced, like a beloved corpse

&

in springmelt. We spent odd weekends relearning what it meant
to be mothered. By then, I was daddy's girl, religion

made me a star, too bright to turn away from.
While I served a Mormon mission,

Mom fell for Kim. While I wrote her letters
about teaching gay couples the law of chastity,

she swanned into a pairing she hid
for a decade.

&

(Lover masquerading as friend, sharing a condo and—I didn't guess—
a bed.) When Mom confessed, a sinkhole

opened my gut, swallowed my orthodoxy slowly. I became Prince
Harry, conscience-pricked by small-mindedness

where before I'd found such
refuge. Or was I now Falstaff to my father's King Henry,

fallen from grace? There I go again. The fat suit and sword
easier than the gnawing, the pang—a canker I can't but worry

&

worse. I was a ten years' blockade. A busy signal.
A poisoned well. My father and his faith I now hold

at arm's length, see its wolf teeth I used to wear, fangs
I didn't know I owned. And now I'm slipping into animal

hide when really there's just this skin,
mine, imperfect, perfectly torn by two continents that thin

a little more each year. I'm closer to my mother than I've ever been.

&

I'm further from my father than I've ever been. There are earthquakes
I can't still. This is my playhouse, its foundation cracked,

its lumber scrubbed clean of ligament till smooth
as driftwood. I perform for the mind a quiet drama,

addicted to happy endings, when reality loops and spirals, serial
tragicomedies jumbled to something in between—ah Hecate—

ripe and sour, flesh and rock, impossible not to
savor the ache, to break and mend and break.

Watching *The Merry Wives of Windsor* with My Girls

Because a glut of glass slippers.

Because a blastoma of pink.

Because Juliet and Ophelia,
yes, but also Anne Page.

Because Anne Page and her decoys,
boys disguised in dresses and veils,
trick away suitors she's
refused. She elopes with *her* pick,
defying both parents.

Because a page to write on
or be written upon.

Because a shortage of girls with ink-stained fingers.

Because Anne authors her own story,
asks forgiveness, not permission.

Because before *Frog and Toad*, there was
Mistress Page and Mistress Ford, sharing letters,
facing snakes. Before Thelma and Louise, these
world-wise women,
watching each other's back.

Because these Merry Wives, friends and tricksters,
specialize in subterfuge, fly
in the face of Falstaff's lewd intentions.

Because a clever mother and clever daughter
grow into—and out of—each other.

Because we coven of sisters
fledge in flocks.

Hecate, as you did for Demeter, do

for these unmothered. Sweep the dead
across the threshold of Dis

into the wings of those who wait,
their talons muddy from the trenches they dug

and filled with wine and flesh to summon
phantom hunger. Suture

Cordelia, Ophelia, Miranda
to their unnamed matrons. Stitch

the rift between Juliet
and Lady C, Perdita

and Hermione. Bring
the mothers of Jessica, Portia, Viola

up from the gut of the earth
into a forest

craquelure with moonlight.
There, in a grotto's mouth,

above a nest of hatchling snakes, set
my mother and me and my daughters. Plant

our feet on an ormolu mount. Interlace
our porcelain. Let incense climb

our limbs and sash
our waists and curl

through our hair in smoky tendrils, unfurling to the stars.

Epilogue—Rosalind with Topophilia and Heresy

I could fall for this low church
        foster forest
pollen in the eyes riming lashes and skin

yellow eucharist
        wild blueberries and huckleberries
grow euphoric

in low scrubs, subalpine
        an august sacrament
of self

-exile, freed from tyranny
        of quotidian, a Sunday
sabbatical your wrestler's

hands testify summer
        wine-colored
our tongues and teeth and lips

I could fall for your
        crouch and grapple
amateur verse inked

by your finger's stylus
        in the hollow of my left thigh
a sanguine pagan

scripture, teach trees your text
        inscribe limerence
in lieu of stone

tablets, valentines
        in roots and veins
of my fleshy tables

benches are for the
        bloodworn, pews
for the pewter-hearted

here we'll indoctrinate
        daughters in blue-
domed sky

seminary their heaven-hunger
        in the baptismal
of a glacial river we'll

mollify here in pine light
        as sun buckles, sun
buckets, through thick hedge

edge along a cliff's hip to forage
        blue fruit we'll scoop
into open mouths

and pails, treebreath loopy,
        our hands stained with
yes

Notes

"Thunder. Enter the three WITCHES *meeting* HECATE*"* is titled after stage directions from *Macbeth*, in which Shakespeare casts Hecate as head witch. In Ancient Greece, Hecate was worshipped as a goddess.

"Self-Portrait as Miranda after Shipwreck" adapts phrases from *The Tempest*. Raised Mormon, the author of this collection was indoctrinated with concepts such as the eternal binary nature of gender and the sinfulness of homosexuality. In 2018, Luke Ramseth states in the *Salt Lake Tribune*, "Suicide is the leading cause of death for Utah youths ages 10 to 17. The state's suicide rate for all ages is more than 60 percent above the national average." California's Prop 8 was a statewide ballot to eliminate the right of same-sex couples to marry. The proposition was aggressively supported by Latter-Day Saint (Mormon) church authorities, who encouraged members to do everything in their power to support the proposition. Prop 8 was approved by voters in November 2008. Two years later, it was deemed unconstitutional and overturned by a federal judge.

"O is the Sound of Tragedy" is titled after a direct quotation from a Shakespeare and Philosophy lecture given by Dr. Mary Janell Metzger.

The first epigraph preceding "Self-Portrait as Cordelia, Mormon Polygamous Wife" is from the journal of Charles Ramsden Bailey, accessed online through Utah State University's historical archive. Charles Ramsden Bailey was born in 1839 in Honley, Yorkshire, England, converted to Mormonism as a boy, and immigrated to Utah in 1855 with his family. He married Susannah Hawkins and Johannah Adamson on the same day, November 7, 1863, and added a third wife, Hannah Jones, seven years later. Altogether, he sired 32 children.

"And Why Not Change the Story?" refers to Banquo as Macbeth's regicidal accomplice, rather than Lady Macbeth. In *Holinshed's Chronicles*, one of Shakespeare's sources for the play, Banquo is implicated in King Duncan's murder, but because King James I claimed to be a descendant of Banquo, Shakespeare rewrote history, most likely to accommodate his powerful patron.

"Self Portrait of Jessica as Mormon Meeting House, Repurposed" includes several stanzas of erasure from standard Mormon texts: the first and thirteenth articles from the Articles of Faith written by Joseph Smith in 1842; verses from a traditional Mormon hymn, "Come, Come Ye Saints," which pioneers sang as they migrated West; the first verse from the Book of Mormon (1 Nephi 1:1); and the baptismal prayer.

"Self-Portrait as Perdita, *Reperta*" alludes to a line from Lucie Brock-Broido's "Noctuary": "Each child still has one lantern inside lit. May the Mother not / Blow her children out."

"After the Curtain Falls, Isabella Speaks in Achromatics" includes a line excerpted from the "Prayer of St. Clare." In *Measure for Measure*, Isabella is training to be a votaress of St. Clare of Assisi. Followers were called "Poor Clares" for their vows of poverty. In the last scene of the play, Vincentio, Duke of Vienna, proposes to Isabella, but Shakespeare doesn't allow her a vocal response.

"Ode to the Plural Marriage of My Mother, Nan Page, Merry Wife, in Five Acts" refers to a 14-year wait before my mother could marry her spouse. Same-sex marriage became legal in Utah for a brief period (December 20, 2013–January 6, 2014), and then again after October 6, 2014, when the United States Supreme Court refused the state of Utah's appeal. My mother and her spouse were married on December 31, 2013.

"Self-Portrait as Miranda with Xenophilia and Apostasy" mentions the Urim and Thummim, which translates literally as "Lights and Perfections." Joseph Smith claimed that he used the Urim and Thummim, two clear stones fastened to a breastplate, to help him translate the Book of Mormon. He also claimed to receive other divine revelations with the help of these stones. The poem also refers to the practice of tarring and feathering, a torture Joseph Smith was once subjected to; the victim would be stripped, doused in pitch, and covered with feathers. The substance was difficult and painful to remove.

"*Thunder and lightning. Enter three* WITCHES" is titled after stage directions from *Macbeth*, and adapts lines from the play. The speakers are based on victims of the North Berwick witch trials (1590–1592), which were instigated by King James I after a perilous sea voyage from Denmark to Scotland. The King was returning from fetching his bride, Anne of Denmark, and he thought witches were behind the storm that almost succeeded in sinking their ship. In 1597, he published *Daemonologie*, a philosophical dissertation on witchcraft, one of Shakespeare's sources for *Macbeth*.

"ab ovo" is from the Latin phrase *ab ovo usque ad mala*, meaning from the egg to the apples. Typically, a Roman meal would begin with eggs, proceed through several courses, and end with apples as dessert. *Ab ovo usque ad mala* became an idiomatic phrase, implying "from the beginning to the end."

"How Not to *Bring Down the Flowers*" incorporates several folk remedies and apotropaic magic, and borrows phrases from Gabrielle Hatfield's *Encyclopedia of Folk Medicine*. "Bringing down the flowers" was a euphemism in early modern England for restoring menstruation, and sometimes referred to causing miscarriage. Hatfield writes, "There were many hundreds of ordinary women who were valued by their communities for their superior knowledge of healing. Shakespeare probably did many of these a disfavor by his portrayal of the witches' brew in Macbeth, an image that has lingered to the present long after we have forgotten the extraordinary *materia medica* in use in official European medicine."

Acknowledgments

I would like to thank the editors of the publications in which these poems first appeared, sometimes in slightly different versions:

AGNI: "O is the Sound of Tragedy"

The American Journal of Poetry: "*Thunder. Enter the three* WITCHES *and* HECATE" and "*Thunder and Lightning. Enter* THREE WITCHES"

Baltimore Review: "Ophelia, Amphibian"

Bellingham Review: "Self-Portrait as Juliet's Nurse with Betta splendens and Pulsar"

Borderline: "Self-Portrait as Miranda, Reminiscent"

Cave Wall: "Self-Portrait as Viola and Olivia in the Gloaming"

Coffin Bell Journal: "Ode to Lady Macbeth," "Hecate, as you did for Demeter, do"

Crab Orchard Review: "Titania in Yellow," "Self-Portrait as Titania, Spellbound"

Dialogue: A Journal of Mormon Thought: "After the Curtain Falls, Isabella Speaks in Achromatics" and "Isabella as Mormon Middle Child"

Flutter Poetry Journal: "Hermione's Statue"

Gingerbread House: "Titania's Adoption Papers," "Self-Portrait as Titania with Cupid's Flower and Changeling" and "Self-Portrait as Titania with Newborn Animus"

Hotel Amerika: "Self-Portrait as Ophelia in 33 Hues of Blewe," "Self-Portrait as Isabella in Theophilic Ecstasy," "Self-Portrait as Rosalind with Topophilia and Heresy," and "Red-Handed"

Matador Review: "How Not to *Bring Down the Flowers*"

Menacing Hedge: "Ode to Paulina"

Mom Egg Review: "Self-Portrait as Lady Macbeth in 30 Shades of Red" and "Gertrude on arte materna"

Passages North: "Self-Portrait as Miranda, A Green Girl"

Red Paint Hill: "Gertrude on artis bene moriendi"

RHINO: "How to Give Birth to Words"

So To Speak: "Self-Portrait as Jessica with Phoropter and Ursa Minor," "Jessica as Mormon Meeting House, Repurposed," "Self-Portrait as Perdita as Lost I," "Portrait of Hermione as Phantom Limn" and "Ode to the Marriage of My Mother, Nan Page, Merry Wife, in Five Acts"

Storyscape Journal: "Anagnorisis—in the Green Room"

Sugar House Review: "Self-Portrait as Miranda After Shipwreck," "Self-Portrait as Cordelia, Mormon Polygamous Wife," "Self-Portrait as Portia and Jessica at the Witching Hour," and "Self-Portrait as Miranda with Xenophilia and Apostasy"

Sweet: "usque ad mala"

Sweet Tree Review: "Self-Portrait as Titania in Hypnopompic Bower"

SWWIM: "Gertrude on artum nuptias"

Tahoma Literary Review: "Self-Portrait as Perdita in 33 Washes of Purple"

Western Humanities Review: "ab ovo" and "Self-Portrait as Perdita, Reperta"

Whale Road Review: "Ode to Juliet"

Zone 3: "Self-Portrait as Perdita with Derelict Ferris Wheel"

Several of these poems appear in the chapbook *Titania in Yellow* (Porkbelly Press, 2019). My sincere gratitude to Nicci Mechler and her team of readers and magic-workers.

My heartfelt thanks to the many poets, professors, editors, classmates, colleagues, and friends who've helped me shape and bring this book to fruition, among them: Bruce Beasley, Tiana Kahakauwila, Kathleen Lundeen, Oliver de la Paz, Susanne Paola Antonetta, Mary Janell Metzger, Evan Mueller, Brenda Miller, Christine Butterworth-McDermott, Star Coulbrooke, Elizabeth Vignali, Jory Mickelson, Megan Spiegel, Jennifer Bullis, Tyler Chadwick, Michael Austin, Rachel Rueckert, Rebecca Beardsall, Marley Simmons-Abril, Katie Weed, Jenny Lara, Fallon Sullivan, Mike Oliphant, Rosemary Engelfried, Elizabeth Cranford Garcia, and the editors at Signature Books.

And to my family, thank you for all your love and support. Nancy and Kim, thank you for teaching me what love is, knocking down all the fences along the way. David and Cherie, thank you for raising me on books and more books. To my siblings, thank you for putting up with me. Charles, thank you for everything. You are my ultimate sounding board. I'm so fortunate to be married to someone who is also thrilled by the Golden Age and has an endless appetite for poetry. Maddie and Lily, you are my heart.

And you, dear reader, thank you for the gift of your time and attention.